DOODLE ART ALLEY BOOKS

EMILY DICKINSON COLORING BOOK • VOLUME 16

Samantha Snyder

Emily Dickinson Coloring Book is available at special discounts when purchased
in quantities for educational use, fundraising, or sales promotions.
For more information, contact: info@akabooks.com

Cover images © 2018 by Doodle Art Alley.
Cover Design by Zaccarine Design, Inc.

"Beauty be not caused—it is" J 516/F 654 – Line 1, "Faith is the pierless bridge" J 915/F 978 – Line 1, "Forever is composed of nows" J 624/F 690 – Line 1, "I dwell in possibility" J 657/F 466 – Line 1, "Luck is not chance" J 1350/F 1360 – Line 1, and "'Nature' is what we see" J 668/F 721 – Line 1 reprinted with permission from THE POEMS OF EMILY DICKINSON: READING EDITION, edited by Ralph W. Franklin, Cambridge, Mass.: The Belknap Press of Harvard University Press, Copyright © 1998 by the President and Fellows of Harvard College. Copyright © 1951, 1955 by the President and Fellows of Harvard College. Copyright © renewed 1979, 1983 by the President and Fellows of Harvard College. Copyright © 1914, 1918, 1919, 1924, 1929, 1930, 1932, 1935, 1937, 1942 by Martha Dickinson Bianchi. Copyright © 1952, 1957, 1958, 1963, 1965 by Mary L. Hampson.

ISBN-13: 978-0998832241
ISBN-10: 0998832243

This edition is published by aka Associates.
www.akabooks.com

Doodle Art Alley Books

Adrift! A little boat adrift!

Emily Dickinson

Doodle Art Alley ©

Beauty be not caused— it is

Emily Dickinson

Doodle Art Alley ©

Faith is a fine invention
~ Emily Dickinson

Doodle Art Alley ©

Faith is the pierless bridge

...Emily Dickinson..

Doodle Art Alley ©

Fame is a bee

Emily Dickinson

Forever is Composed of Nows

Emily Dickinson

Doodle Art Alley ©

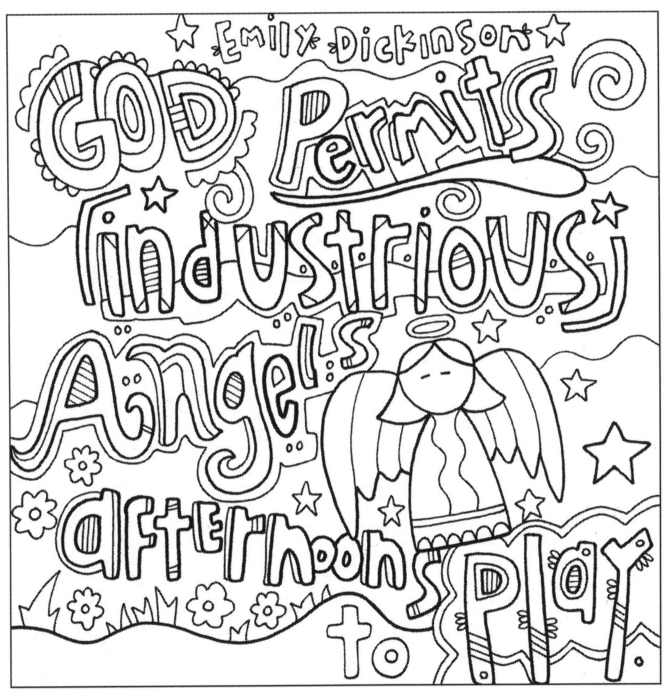

Emily Dickinson

God Permits Industrious Angels Afternoons to Play

Hope is the thing with feathers
That perches in the soul,
And sings the tune withoutthe words,
And never stops at all,

And sweetest in the gale is heard;
And sore must be the storm
That could abash the little bird
That kept so many warm.

I've heard it in the chillest land,
And on the strongest sea;
Yet, never, in extremity,
It asked a crumb of me.

-Emily Dickinson

Doodle Art Alley

Hope is the thing with feathers that perches in the soul

Emily Dickinson

Doodle Art Alley ©

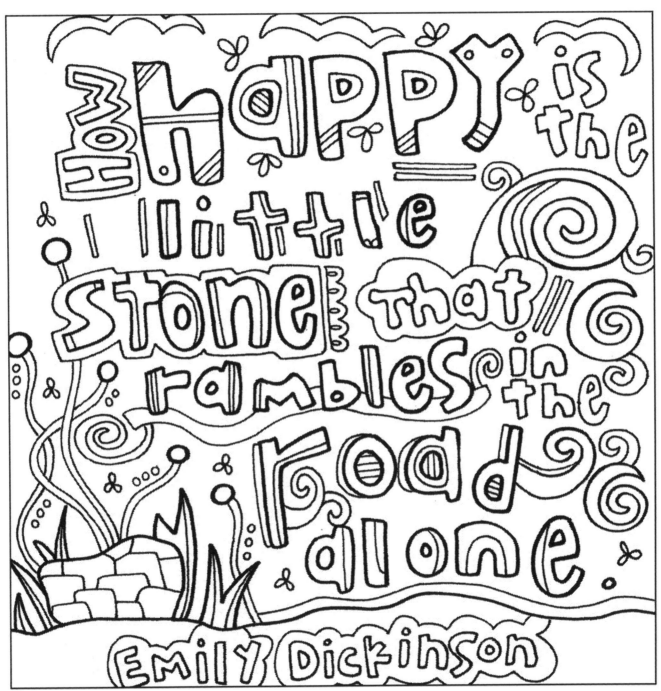

How Happy is the little stone that rambles in the road alone.

Emily Dickinson

Doodle Art Alley ©

I dwell in Possibility

Emily Dickinson

Doodle Art Alley ©

If I can Stop one heart from breaking, I shall not live in Vain.
Emily Dickinson

Doodle Art Alley ©

I'll tell you how the sun rose, -
A ribbon at a time.
The steeples swam in amethyst.
The news like squirrels ran.

The hills untined their bonnets.
The bobolinks begun.
Then I said softly to myself,
"That must have been the sun!"

But how he set, I know not.
There seemed a purple stile
Which little yellow boys and girls
Were climbing all the while

Till when they reached the other side.
A dominie in gray
Put gently up the evening bars,
And led the flock away.

-Emily Dickinson

Doodle Art Alley ©

I'll tell you how the Sun rose, A ribbon at a Time

Emily Dickinson

I'm nobody! Who are you?
Are you nobody, too?
Then there's a pair of us - don't tell!
They'd banish us, you know.

How dreary to be somebody!
How public, like a frog
To tell your name the livelong day
To an admiring bog!

-Emily Dickinson

I'M NOBODY! WHO ARE YOU?

...EMILY DICKINSON...

Doodle Art Alley ©

This is my letter to the world,
That never wrote to me, -
The simple news that Nature told,
With tender majesty.

Her message is committed
To the hands I cannot see;
For love of her, sweet countrymen,
Judge tenderly of me!

-Emily Dickinson

Doodle Art Alley ©

Judge tenderly of me!

Emily Dickinson

Doodle Art Alley ©

Look back on time with kindly eyes, he doubtless did his best. Emily Dickinson

Doodle Art Alley ©

Luck is not chance
Emily Dickinson

Much madness is divinest sense
To a discerning eye;
Mush sense the startkest madness.
'Tis the majority
In this, as all, prevails.
Assent, and you are sane;
Demur, - you're straightway dangerous,
And handled with a chain.

-Emily Dickinson

Emily Dickinson

Much Madness is divinest Sense to a discerning eye

Doodle Art Alley ©

My friend must be a bird because it flies!

Emily Dickinson

Doodle Art Alley ©

nature is what we see

EMILY DICKINSON

Doodle Art Alley ©

Doodle Art Alley ©

Success is counted sweetest
By those who ne'er succeed.
To comprehend a nectar
Requires sorest need.

Not one of all the purple host
Who took the flag today
Can tell the definition,
So clear, of victory,

As he, defeated, dying,
On whose forbidden ear
The distant strains of triumph
Break, agonized and clear.

-Emily Dickinson

Doodle Art Alley ©

Success is Counted Sweetest by those who ne'er Succeed

Emily Dickinson

Doodle Art Alley ©

The brain is wider than the sky,
For, put them side by side,
The one the other will include
With ease, and you beside.

The brain is deeper than the sea,
For, hold them, blue to blue,
The one the other will absorb,
As sponges, buckets do.

The brain is just the weight of God,
For, lift them, pound for pound,
And they will differ, if they do,
As syllable from sound.

-Emily Dickinson

Doodle Art Alley ©

The brain is wider than the sky. -Emily Dickinson

Emily Dickinson

The Skies can't keep their secret!

The soul selects her own society,
Then shuts the door;
On her divine majority
Present no more.

Unmoved, she notes the chariot's pausing
At her low gate;
Unmoved, an emperor be kneeling
Upon her mat.

I've known her from an ample nation
Choose one;
Then close the valves of her attention
Like Stone.

-Emily Dickinson

Doodle Art Alley ©

The Soul selects her own Society Then Shuts the door.

Emily Dickinson

The Soul should always stand Ajar.

Emily Dickinson

Doodle Art Alley ©

Doodle Art Alley ©

There is no frigate like a book
To take us lands away,
Nor any coursers like a page
of prancing poetry.

This traverse may the poorest take
Without oppress of toll;
How frugal is the chariot
That bears the human soul!

-Emily Dickinson

Doodle Art Alley ©

There is no Frigate like a book to take us lands away.

EMILY DICKINSON

Doodle Art Alley ©

There's a certain slant of light on winter afternoons. Emily Dickinson

Doodle Art Alley ©

To hear an Oriole sing May be a Common thing, or only all divine.

Emily Dickinson

Doodle Art Alley ©

To live is so startling it leaves little time for anything else

Emily Dickinson

Doodle Art Alley ©

Truth is such a rare thing it is delightful to tell it.

Emily Dickinson

Doodle Art Alley ©

Two butterflies went out at noon and waltzed above a stream

Emily Dickinson

We never know how High we are Till we are called to rise.

Emily Dickinson

Doodle Art Alley ©

We turn not Older with tears, but newer every day.

Emily Dickinson

Doodle Art Alley ©

Wild nights! Wild nights!
Were I with thee,
Wild nights should be
Our luxury!

Futile the winds
To a heart in port, ~
Done with the compass,
Done with the chart.

Rowing in Eden!
Ah! the sea!
Might I but moor
Tonight in thee!

-Emily Dickinson

Doodle Art Alley

Emily Dickinson

Wild nights! Wild nights!

You've seen balloons set, haven't you?

Emily Dickinson

Doodle Art Alley ©

Doodle Art Alley ©

Doodle Art Alley ©

Doodle Art Alley ©

Doodle Art Alley ©

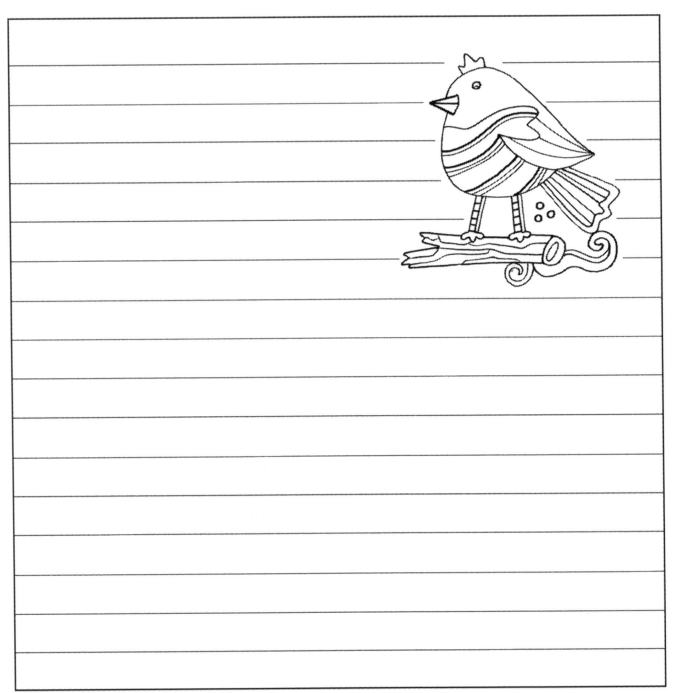

Doodle Art Alley ©

Doodle Art Alley ©

Doodle Art Alley ©

Doodle Art Alley ©

Emily Dickinson
December 10, 1830 ~ May 15, 1886

Emily Dickinson was an American poet. Although extremely prolific in her writings, shewas not publicly recognized during her lifetime. After her death, her younger sister, Lavinia, discovered 40 hand-bound volumes of nearly 1,800 poems. The first volume of her work was published in 1890, but it wasn't until 1955 that a complete collection of her poetry was prepared by Thomas H. Johnson for publication by Harvard University Press as *The Poems of Emily Dickinson*.

The most recent editions of Emily Dickinson's poetry and letters include *The Poems of Emily Dickinson*, edited by R. W. Franklin, 1998; *The Poems of Emily Dickinson*, edited by Thomas Johnson,1955; and *The Letters of Emily Dickinson*, edited by Thomas Johnson, 1958. Early editions of Dickinson's work are now in the public domain. These editions include those edited by Mabel Loomis Todd and Thomas Wentworth Higginson in the 1890s, as well as some of Martha Dickinson Bianchi's editions.

Known for using unorthodox punctuation, rhythm, and syntax throughout her poetry, Dickinson didn't follow the traditional rules of the genre. She is considered to be one of the most significant American poets of all time.

Doodle Art Alley ©

ABOUT DOODLE ART ALLEY

Samantha Snyder is the author of more than 20 award-winning and best-selling coloring books in the Doodle Art Alley Books series including *Attitude Is Everything, Believe in Yourself, Imagination Will Take You Everywhere,* and *Mistakes Are Proof That You Are Trying.*

She has been doodling her whole life. While teaching elementary school, she often drew up coloring pages and printables for her students and fellow teachers. She decided to start sharing her creations and in 2008, Doodle Art Alley was founded.

A quick glance at a doodle may show scribbles, random lines and shapes with no meaning or significance. However, with a little love and direction, these drawings have the potential to compete with some of the best artwork there is!

Doodle Art Alley is dedicated to giving those squiggly lines the proper credit they deserve. Who would have thought that such a small and simple idea could possess so much potential?

There are lots of fun doodle art activities, tips, and information to read through and enjoy. Visit **www.doodle-art-alley.com** for hundreds of exciting doodles.

Doodle Art Alley Books

Made in the USA
Middletown, DE
21 January 2022

59318021R00075